50 Quotes From Empowering Women That Could Change Your Mindset

By: April P. Cooper

Edited By: Tienne Weyer

Weyer Publishers

Stockton, California 95209

ISBN-13: 978-0615481180

For more information or to order additional books, please contact:

Weyer Publishers
9827 Koala Court
Stockton, CA 95209
wweyer@weyerpublishers.net
www.weyerpublishers.net

Acknowledgements

As this text in its entirety is designed to acknowledge the changes others have made in me, I want to be sure to acknowledge the two women whom have affected my life the most drastically in order to inspire these words. First and foremost is my mother, Ms. Arnetta Jane Moore, for without your sacrifice, guidance, patience, tolerance, acceptance and teaching I would not be the woman I am today. The other would be, Mrs. Inez Aldridge. You have been my support in near sisterly pursuit. Your guidance has never failed to come to my aid during the most turbulent and confusing times when it is needed most. Not only am I happy to have you both in my life, but I have no idea where I would be in this world without either of you or your influences. Thank you for inspiring me. Thank you for guiding me. Thank you and I love you always.

April

Foreword

Change always starts somewhere. In my life, I've had lots of it. From that strenuous transition from little girl to woman all the way down to living in a strange world that often times seems to challenge my physical, mental, emotional, and spiritual perceptions.

I just don't understand why life decisions have to be so complicated or how I'm supposed to resolve my spiritual with the physical world I've been chained to that in so many ways contradicts my faith and encourages me to question it.

To me, the most important attribute I credit my faith with is simply the ideal that if you give to the world then you will receive blessings beyond the imagination of any man. I've done this so many times with individuals and have had my good hearted nature thrown back in my face. I've had women who claim to truly believe in equality of man and the need for women to stand together united in order to accomplish even the smallest of things turn right around and tell me that they don't have the time to invest in me...my plight...my hope...or my dream...even though I have helped these same women with theirs so many times before.

I see this not only as a slight against me, but a slap in the face to that beautiful thing called friendship that I extended to them. I also see these kinds of acts as a work of something otherworldly meant to discourage me from pushing forward and through.

The words of great women in history are what have helped me through this disheartening ordeal. They are what have helped me stay true to me and concentrate on a goal instead of bitterness. Here, I want to continue their work and share with you those thoughts and quotations that have helped me see who I am...in spite of any label others may place on me...and stay true to that.

These women have taught me to face adversity and how to go about that. They have taught me the application of ideals. They have taught me to love...my husband...my children...my God...and most importantly...to love myself as I am.

I won't allow their teachings to be lost or tainted by hatefulness or a lack of resolve. Here, I'm sharing my resolve and hopefully continuing their work. Not only are these things important to women as a unit, but also as individuals.

"I've always believed that one woman's success can only help another woman's success."

-Gloria Vanderbilt

What the quote by Gloria Vanderbilt means to me and why I picked this one from many is the fact that it talks about helping other women. And that is what I feel living and networking is REALLY all about. I feel strongly that women should teach each other how to be successful the right way in order to increase their life and their blessings. In order for us all to have an opportunity at success, we should be giving those opportunities as freely as we want to receive them.

"The especial genius of women I believe to be electrical in movement, intuitive in function, and spiritual in tendency."

-Margaret Fuller

Margaret Fullers quote is another one where certain words in this particular quote resonate with me. For instance: Genius, Electrical, Intuitive, and Spiritual. These words I take as smart energy that is aware of anything and centered within our heart and soul. The reason I think this is important to ALL women is that it is important on many levels to combine our minds, bodies, and spirits in order to accomplish even the simplest of tasks.

"There is a special place in hell for women who do not help other women."

-Madeleine K. Albright

This quote fortunately does not need further explanation. I feel that she was straight forward and shot from the hip on this topic. I can agree with her on this because we all are supposed to help and teach each other without having envy or jealousy. One woman's turn for success today means more room for another woman's success tomorrow!

"Women are the real architects of society."

-Harriet Beecher Stowe

When you think about it, women are the heart beat, we are the pen, and we are the ink. We are the tools used to further our society. Although the men like to take all of the credit for the building of everything, they could not have built any of it without our support. We ARE what gives our society structure. We are the ones who teach the children, and groom the up and coming leaders of our communities. In a sense, we are the support beams that hold all of the buildings together. There is no doubt in my mind that without us, it would all quickly crumble away.

"Remember, Ginger Rogers did everything Fred Astaire did, but she did it backwards and in high heels."

-Faith Whittlesey

When I read this quote, I think of Grace. Now when you think about it...high heels and backwards...not only did this woman manage to accomplish and not just be "as good as" but "better than" a man at this, but she did it while still remaining a lady, a woman, a role model, AND did it all making it seem effortless. I think as women there is nothing we can't achieve just as long as we help each other along the way.

"I am a woman above everything else."

-Jacqueline Kennedy Onassis

A lady with style and finesse was Mrs. Jacqueline Kennedy-Onasis. In spite of some of the more difficult things this woman had to deal with...situations where most of us would be quite tempted to reduce ourselves to bad behavior in order to simply cope with the issues...Jackie always held her head up high as well as held herself to a higher standard. She just screamed what a woman should look like and act like when you present yourself in public. Being a woman above anything else is correct. Nothing too much over the top or too little, it was all just right.

"I have yet to hear a man ask for advice on how to combine marriage and a career."

-Gloria Steinem

We as women have a rather nasty habit of thinking we are "Super Woman." We somehow think we can do it all...leap tall buildings with a single bound and still make it home in time to make dinner and do laundry. As women, we seem to want to "combine" EVERYTHING with our careers. In this regard we have much to learn from men. We need to learn to take care of ourselves and nurture our own dreams. A dream is not something insignificant that can easily be brushed aside without brushing aside a part of who we are as women. Without dreams, we are nothing but empty shells of people...incomplete.

"As a woman, I find it very embarrassing to be in a meeting and realize that I'm the only one in the room with balls."

-Rita Mae Brown

This quote means to me that sometimes it takes a woman to be a "man" and stand up to take a stand. What's more unfortunate is that they call this kind of an act "being a man" yet it is usually the woman that not only has the balls, but also the fortitude, arrogance, and downright tenacity to see the issues through to the end.

"You have to recognize when the right place and the right time fuse and take advantage of the opportunity. There are plenty of opportunities out there. You can't sit back and wait."

-Ellen Metcalf

Reading this quote reminds me of telling women to get up off of their butt and stop waiting for a man to do something for you when you are perfectly capable of getting it done yourself. Furthermore, usually when a woman does something herself, she does a better and more efficient job than a man could ever dream of doing. Women have excelled in more things than men...so...what exactly are you waiting for?

"I believe in prayer. It's the best way we have to draw strength from heaven."

-Josephine Baker

Driving...I can't think of a better reason to pray. I don't know how many times I've called out from behind the wheel of my Yukon..."Jesus, please stop me from rolling down this window...Jesus, please help me to have the strength not to ram this crazy man with my truck and show him what 4x4 is...Thank you Jesus." Thankfully, the lord has always answered my prayers. God has the power to move mountains...goodness knows I'm a mountain to move all on my own.

"Life is short and it's up to you to make it sweet."

-Sadie Delany

This tells me that I should work at making my life sweet. Life being short...not a whole lot any of us can do about that one...it's already been taken care of. Making life pleasant is quite a task and it should be a task we are all eager to fulfill. It takes too much energy to stay mad all of the time...why not invest that energy in ensuring that your life is as pleasant as possible. I say we should all show some love to anyone and everyone we meet. Yes...even the one you just questioned from that little voice in your head!

"I used to want the words "She Tried" on my tombstone. Now I want "She Did It."

-Katherine Dunham

This quote says to me that I should live my life to the fullest and make sure to put my personal stamp on this world everywhere I go. I take this quote to heart...and I'm doing it moving!

"I am not tragically colored. There is no great sorrow dammed up in my soul, nor lurking behind my eyes...even in the Helter-Skelter skirmish that is my life, I have seen that the world is to the strong regardless of a little pigmentation more or less. No, I do not weep at the world-I am too busy sharpening my oyster knife."

-Zora Neale Hurston

Zora says A LOT in this quote, but what it says to me is that I need to ignore the negative motivators and look forward instead of pondering backwards. There will always be those people that will attempt to distract me from my goals by way of influencing me negatively and encouraging me to pay heed to past obstacles that there is nothing I can do to change instead of helping me stay focused on the issues and obstacles in front of me that I still have the power and presence of mind to handle. I need to ignore these types of people and actively seek out those who will assist and encourage positive management of these things. Sharpen that Oyster knife...ALWAYS!

"Defining myself, as opposed to being defined by others, is one of the most difficult challenges I face."

-Carol Moseley-Braun

Oh my God!!!! This quote is one that I deal with every day because defining yourself is hard. For me, this has been one of my biggest challenges that I struggle with still to this very day. It is easy to define the negative things about a person especially yourself because you will always get help from others in that regard. People will always try to paint their own picture of you. I say, you have two choices...let someone paint the picture and buy it or say screw it and pick up a paint brush and start painting your own self-portrait!

"Sometimes you've got to let everything go-purge yourself. If you are unhappy with anything...whatever is bringing you down, get rid of it. Because you'll find that when you're free, your true creativity, your true self comes out."

-Tina Turner

I love this lady Tina Turner. I hope when I get up there in age that the energy she has, I still have at least 75% of it when I'm out and about on the stage. When I'm out there on stage or wherever I'm privileged to be so that I may pass my thoughts and my words on to another young woman and have the passion to express the importance of what I KNOW at this point in my life to be true.

"I still have my feet on the ground, I just wear better shoes."

-Oprah Winfrey

You know, I may not agree with this lady on some things, but I do know that she is an excellent "giver." Her quote tells me that in spite and because of my success I always need to remember to be humble, but also make sure to be knowledgeable as well. It also says that maybe you have to change your location as your pockets increase but never to change the loving person you are and never forget where I came from!

"I had to make my own living and my own opportunity. But I made it! Don't sit down and wait for the opportunities to come. Get up and make them."

-Madam C.J. Walker

This woman was amazing to be wealthy during that time both financially and intellectually. This quote of many tells me every day to make sure my butt doesn't sit around waiting for opportunities to come to me, but to make them myself by being in the right place at the right time. It also tells me that I may have to MAKE my right place and time by being the tenacious and aggressive woman I was born to be.

"Freeing yourself was one thing; claiming ownership of that freed self was another."

-Toni Morrison

By reading this quote, it makes me feel that when I'm to claim ownership of something, that my belief rises within myself. I truly have the freedom to do what I want just as long as it helps people, especially other women.

"Don't wait around for other people to be happy for you. Any happiness you get you've got to make yourself."

-Alice Walker

This quote is one of those inner-success techniques that I have to challenge myself to do each day. I have come to find out in my life that I can be happy all by myself, but of course the "word of the lord" keeps me happy to know that He is with me. Although many people profess to believe in the "word," I have found that jealousy is more prevalent that I ever thought possible. I have found that when others have success they expect you to root and cheer them on, but rarely have I ever found that (even when I am the first to give this) is it ever reciprocated. I won't ever let anyone stop me from cheering...for myself...or better yet for others!

"I have learned over the years that when one's mind is made up, this diminishes fear; knowing what must be done does away with fear."

-Rosa Parks

What I have learned from this is that if I make up my mind to do something I must have a plan in place in order to see it through to the end. This also tells me that fear can be and is my worst enemy and it is not just my job, but my duty to overcome my fear in order to realize my goals and prevent anything or anyone from standing in my way of success.

"Without faith, nothing is possible. With it, nothing is impossible."

-Mary McLeod Bethune

I agree wholeheartedly on this one. When I think of faith I think of an unbreakable and untouchable force that protects me so long as I hold firm to it. In the spare moment it takes for my faith to falter, it only takes a fraction of that time for my protection from the external elements that are meant to distract or destroy me to be allowed to enter into my existence. The results of applying this concept in my life have flourished beyond even my own imagination. I think, believe, and feel that this is largely due to my faith and the direction I receive as a result of my dedication to it.

"If the first woman God ever made was strong enough to turn the world upside down all alone, these together ought to be able to turn it back and get it right-side up again."

-Sojourner Truth

This quote is one that has me thinking about how it would be great if all women would come together and protest or fight for what is right both positive and meaningful. We would be further along than we are now.

"Our work has only begun. In our time we have an historic opportunity to shape a global balance of power that favors freedom and that will therefore deepen and extend the peace. And I use the word power broadly, because even more important than military and indeed economic power is the power of ideas, the power of compassion, and the power of hope."

-Condoleezza Rice

This woman is powerful and will not back down to the media or any questions that may come her way. This quote represents "power." I love how she speaks about power and also how she is talking about a balance for the entire world. The focus on the world is largely important to me to bring our focus down to humanity instead one single government or society. Why? Because it is the first step needed to happen in order to promote steps toward world peace.

"There never will be complete equality until women themselves help to make laws and elect lawmakers."

-Susan B. Anthony

This quote had me at "complete equality." How many places in the world actually have this now? Although women make up more than half of the population of the world, we make up less than half of the law makers and politicians in the United States alone, which has more women in political positions than any other country in the world per capita. So ladies, we have A LOT of work to do still. So get off of the men's coat tails and come to join the Change movement!

"For what is done or learned by one class of woman becomes, by virtue of their common womanhood, the property of all women."

-Elizabeth Blackwell

This quote was one of the ones that SHOULD motivate women to move forward. This can be accomplished by the simple sharing of knowledge on their methods of being successful so that we can all share in the feeling that comes with success no matter how great or small. We've gotten stuck on this idea of "class." It is as though the amount of money we are in possession of somehow makes us more or less worthy of knowledge. As they say, "knowledge is power." Let us focus on empowering each other. It is this simple empowerment that will lead us into a new and changed world. Simple acts is all it takes to be a part of "global change."

"We've chosen the path to equality; don't let them turn us around."

-Geraldine Ferraro

Here we go again with the word equality. To me that should be a clue. That is why I am involved in helping women evolve into their butterfly, so we all can move forward instead of backwards.

"You can do one of two things; just shut up, which is something I don't find easy, or learn an awful lot very fast, which is what I tried to do."

-Jane Fonda

This lady is just funny to me, but her quote struck me because of the "learn an awful lot very fast" which is something I'm used to getting. My whole life, I feel that I've been expected to learn everything faster than is reasonable. I think as women we are expected to somehow be "perfect." We're expected to handle even the most difficult of circumstances and all with a smile upon our beautiful faces. We're expected to "restrain" ourselves. We're expected to control our emotions. God forbid we cry. God forbid we love. But only when it is convenient for others. I say damn their inconvenience. If something hurts cry. If something moves you...for heaven's sake SAY SO!

"If you have knowledge, let others light their candles in it."

-Margaret Fuller

Knowledge is something that I find to be very important. As they say "knowledge is power." It is our duty as women to empower each other and ensure that no one is ever allowed to keep us in the dark again. I don't understand this idea that some people have to keep all of their knowledge to themselves. I just don't understand why it is so important for them to deny an education to another person. It is almost as though they feel superior for knowing something that the rest of the world doesn't. Somehow, the simple act of them being in possession of this "secret" empowers them. They should feel more empowered by simply letting others in on the "secret."

"My address is like my shoes. It travels with me. I abide where there is a fight against wrong."

-Mother Jones

This quote makes me feel that I am doing the right thing by fighting against anything that is wrongfully done towards anyone, but especially toward women. It also reminds me that wherever I go, I take myself with me so I always remember that my "address" is quite literally IN my shoes...I'll never shake my address so I'd better work at making it a desirable location!

"Don't compromise yourself.
You are all you've got."

-Janis Joplin

I agree so much with this quote because the meaning of it is that you are unique and you need to take care of you before you focus on taking care of others. So ladies while you are out there in this confusing and treacherous world, remember, you are unique and don't ever compromise who you are to make others happy.

"Many persons have a wrong idea of what constitutes true happiness. It is not attained through self-gratification but through fidelity to a worthy purpose."

-Helen Keller

Self gratification is not the path to true happiness. When we use the word fidelity, many people use this word only in reference to marriage or relationships. My vision is this...everyone is in a relationship with themselves. Our "id" is constantly in a proverbial war with our ego and they are required to coexist for the duration of our life. This causes an internal confusion which we need to strive to subside in any way we can. I say fidelity is not a religious issue or an issue solely for external relationships. We need to apply this word and live it as though it were a way of life, because it is. Ask this one question of yourself...what gives me self worth? Honor that answer and be loyal to it as you would expect another to honor and be loyal to you. If it is worth your time to give your loyalty to another person, don't you think an idea you hold dear deserves the same respect?

"If we are to achieve a richer culture, rich in contrasting values, we must recognize the whole gamut of human potentialities, and so weave a less arbitrary social fabric, one in which each diverse gift will find a fitting place."

-Margaret Mead

I love the idea of our social structure being compared to a fabric. It makes me think of the good old days when women spent their time sewing patchwork quilts. It reminds me of a time in which women had TRUE partnership and gave of themselves freely to other women in an effort to support their entire community. Each woman was responsible for a portion of the quilt, but if she needed help she never feared to ask another for it. We need to get back to that time. We need to find our "fitting place." We need to assist another in finding their "fitting place." We also need to find a way to be happy for one another when we each find our respective "fitting places" because they all complement each other. Just like a patchwork quilt, if you take one patch out, it ruins the entire masterpiece.

"Something which we think is impossible now is not impossible in another decade."

-Constance Baker Motley

I am reminded here of Galileo Galilei. When he invented the first telescope he was written off as a crazy witchcraft practitioner. He was even brought before a council where he was judged to be insane. Just 3 decades ago, it was thought impossible for a woman to be qualified enough to run for president. Today, telescopes are commonly sold at nearly any store and used by even the most advanced research facilities to study the stars. What's more is that a woman becoming president is just a stone's throw away. This tells me that it is my responsibility to be part of the coming change. The change may not happen today, tomorrow, or the day after that, but the change is coming. The only way for the change to happen is for people to get on board with the change...and MAKE it happen!

"Never doubt that a small group of thoughtful committed citizens can change the world. Indeed, it is the only thing that ever has."

-Margaret Mead

At this moment, I'm reminded of the beginnings of nearly every government action that has ever taken place in the world. Jesus Christ (just to name one of many) began with just a few followers (12 to be exact) dedicated to a particular cause. It didn't take long for the 12 to grow to thousands and convert into a "movement." From there, less than 200 years is what it took to begin the world change to what we see today in Christianity. The women's movement began in a similar fashion. Just a small group of women who have grown into the millions we see today focused on a global change. Alone, I am just one woman. With my sisters joined together, we are millions, we are the majority. Let's join together and try to accomplish even a fraction of what Jesus did...let's focus on a global change!

"I think the key is for women not to set any limits."

-Martina Navratilova

Society in general puts many limits on women. We are limited by our gender alone as though an extra appendage between our legs would make our minds somehow work better. When you come into a world that already has preconceived notions on who or what you are going to be, your best bet is to not set any more for yourself. So, make it so...the sky is the limit!

"Remember no one can make you feel inferior without your consent."

-Eleanor Roosevelt

Amen! Halleluiah! Tell it sister! Oooh! I can NOT say enough about this quote! By allowing others to influence you, your feelings, and your thoughts, you are giving your consent to be controlled. We, as women, have been fighting for our freedom for centuries. Why do we now give the control back to those people who obviously do not know how to control themselves? Take the control back! Be in control of not only who you are, but also what you are and how you feel about whom and what you are. We need to feel empowered by who we are and we need to empower others as well.

"The first problem for all of us, women, is not to learn, but to unlearn."

-Gloria Steinem

Lord, if I see another woman who doesn't understand this quote, please come down and stop me from putting my hands on them! We as women have been predisposed to the WORST possible upbringing. Much like a convict being released from prison after a 35 year stretch, we women have to unlearn all that our mothers have taught us. At this moment I'm having a flash back of Whoopie Goldberg as a nun singing "if you want to be somebody, if you want to go somewhere, you gotta stand up and pay attention." There is no better advice than this. We, as women, need to stand up and pay attention and stop perpetuating the foul teachings we have been burdened with and passing them right on down to our young women. Stop! Be the change! Let our young women live our new world! Turn their uphill battle into a cross-country jog!

"It's so clear that you have to cherish everyone. I think that's what I get from these older black women that every soul is to be cherished, that every flower is to bloom."

-Alice Walker

A friend of mine once told me that someone had compared her to a Lotus flower. For this particular woman, I thought that analogy to be quite fitting. A Lotus flower both blooms and seeds at the same time whilst growing out of muck and filth. This friend, like many women I know, has done just that. She blooms and rejuvenates no matter how much filth you put on her and gets even more beautiful with each cycle. See, what others don't realize is that maneuver may stink, but it is the healthiest way I know of to ensure that whatever lesson there is to learn is solidified in a mind.

"As a woman I have no country. As a woman my country is the whole world."

-Virginia Woolf

I thought this quote to be very prophetic and true on SO many levels. The thing is we put so much stock into property lines and belonging to a nation that we forget what the purpose for us being here is. The fact is...God does not have property lines...He owns everything! Therefore, we as a people own nothing because in truth, it all belongs to God. If we put more stock into humanity than we do nationality, race, gender, or anything else for that matter...I think we'd be far better off. Really, in reading the good word that is what I take from it is that we are here to take care of one another (including our land) but above all one another.

"I've learned from experience that the greater part of our happiness or misery depends on our dispositions and not on our circumstances."

-Martha Washington

When you think about this, it really hits you in the gut. Generally speaking, we tend to allow our negative circumstances affect our mentality in negative ways. Now, you would think that we would also allow our positive circumstances affect us, but that is almost never the case. You hear all of these stories of really fantastic people making changes in the world that came from hovels of nothingness, but made the best of it. It wasn't their circumstances that pushed them forward...it was their overall disposition and mentality. If we all could hold on to that positive disposition, I feel it clear down to my bones that we would be capable of overcoming anything!

"Follow your instincts-you never know if your ideas will work out unless you try them."

-Lulu Guinness

Fear has always been a big one for me. I'm afraid of myself...really. Maybe it's fear of success, fear of accomplishment, all I know for sure is that it is definitely fear that has held me back for so long. So, I never tried. So, I always failed, BECAUSE I never tried anything new. Today, I'm no longer afraid of myself, success, or accomplishment. Today, I'm not trying...Today, I'm doing!

"Just don't give up trying to do what you really want to do. Where there is love and inspiration, I don't think you can go wrong."

-Ella Fitzgerald

People. People have always been another of my biggest challenges...especially people with negative intentions. I've never understood why others don't have the need to inspire others the way I do. Most of the people I've met are exactly the opposite. They feel the need to drag you down and impede your progress in some way. It's almost as though they feel that by you succeeding you are somehow leaving them behind. I don't know about everyone else, but I want to bring those who lifted me up along for the ride. Maybe it's selfish, but I just hope they'll keep on lifting me up...their encouragement is what got me there in the first place.

"Life is a succession of moments. To live each one is to succeed."

-Corita Kent

Wow, don't I know it. I've lived this quote so many times; I don't think I would be able to explain it in just a few short sentences. Simply living is a challenge for me. There are so many dichotomies in my perceptions of the world around me, often times even my faith can't hold me. The only thing I can do is just break down and cry. But then, my faith kicks in and lifts me up so that I can go out and do it all again.

"Play keeps us vital and alive.
It gives us an enthusiasm for
life that is irreplaceable.
Without it, life just doesn't
taste good."

-Lucia Capocchione

I just finished talking to a friend about this. She's a musician and often time's people reduce her work to "JUST entertainment." Without music, pictures, paintings, sculptures, and performance arts of all kinds...where would we be? Even writing is a form of expression. Being able to say things you wouldn't normally be able to express verbally. Either because of fear of rejection for having the thoughts/feelings or just simply not having the ability to say it in the way it needs to be said to truly express an idea. Entertainment is a vital key to keeping us healthy physically, emotionally, and spiritually.

"Respect....is appreciation of the separateness of the other person, of the way in which she is unique."

-Annie Gottlieb

You know, it's really very easy to respect someone's beliefs or even respect them as an individual when they agree with you. What's hard is respecting someone when their point of view differs from your own. I really like the fact that I have friends whose opinions vary so vastly from my own because it gives me an opportunity to delve into other possible understandings of life and the world. I think our world in and of itself would be very boring if we each did not possess one firm little piece of uniqueness. Just as I want others to respect those things about me that make me unique, I need to respect and appreciate those qualities about them as well. I don't have to LIKE those things, but I do need to respect and appreciate them.

"The beauty of empowering others is that your own power is not diminished in the process."

-Barbara Coloroso

I'm always perplexed by the insurmountable number of women who just do NOT understand this statement. Empowering others actually empowers YOU! It makes you a small part of whatever they are doing and thus makes you part of their ultimate success. My attitude is that one can only be successful with a small group of supporters backing them. Ideally, you have a small network of people who simply give encouragement and support to one another. The product of this act is simple...everyone has the opportunity to succeed and no one get's "left behind."

"I don't mind living in a man's world so long as I get to be a woman in it."

-Marilyn Monroe

I have a friend who is a writer and someone
gave her a bad review. It was obvious that
the review was more personal in nature
than about her book. She simply smiled
and responded to the remark. Really, I had
to giggle at her response. She thanked the
person for the nasty review. When I asked
her why she did that, she replied,"If I had
responded negatively it would have given
them exactly what they wanted. By
smiling in their face and behaving
myself, I may as well have whipped them
with a switch...saying thank you is often
worse than telling them off." This woman
has a way of saying thank you or "I'm so
sorry you feel that way" so sweetly and
with a smile on her face, but you know
EXACTLY what she means. Being a lady
can sometimes be more empowering than
being a b****.

"Self-love has very little to do with how you feel about your outer self. It`s about accepting all of yourself. You`ve got to learn to accept the fool in you as well as the part that`s got it goin` on."

-Tyra Banks

How do you REALLY go about loving yourself? I still haven't figured that one out completely. But, I think this Tyra girl has explained it perfectly. We're all intelligent to some degree, but we're also all fools to some degree as well. The great purpose of it all is to not let the guilt kill you when the fool presents herself. We're better off accepting the fact that we are imperfect and it is our imperfections that makes each of us so unique and thus so loveable.

"Don't settle for average. Bring your best to the moment. Then, whether it fails or succeeds, at least you know you gave all you had. We need to live the best that's in us."

-Angela Bassett

I've struggled with this my entire life. I see these women who will attempt to hold me back. My attitude is, if you're going to 'bring it' bring it ALL! Don't do anything half-way. A friend reminded me of her Girl Scouts troop slogan. "What you have is God's gift to you. What you do with what you have is your gift to God." God doesn't give frivolously. He gives with intent and reason that although unknown to us has a well thought out plan. If God asked you for a glass of water, would you serve it to him in a dirty cup? Most likely you wouldn't, so then why do you serve the world the gifts He has given to you on a filthy platter?

"What do you do when disappointment comes? When it weighs on you like a rock, you can either let it press you down until you become discouraged, even devastated, or you can use it as a stepping-stone to better things."

-Joyce Meyer

Disappointment is a relative term to say the least. I like this idea of using disappointment as a stepping stone. It really brings reality to a situation and in some ways some clarity. We all suffer disappointment at one time or another, but are you willing to let one small disappointment distract you from your goal? I'd say not. I say, let that little bit or even large rocks of disappointment evolve into the fuel for your success. Make that disappointment catapult you forward into the life or situation you ultimately desire.

50 Quotes From Empowering Women

CONTACT

April P. Cooper
10940 Trinity Parkway, Ste C-161
Stockton, Ca 95219
888-578-6398 Ext.6

http://www.aprilpcooper.com
info@aprilpcooper.com

www.ingramcontent.com/pod-product-compliance
Lightning Source LLC
Chambersburg PA
CBHW060356050426
42449CB00009B/1753